Every Day's a Dog's Day

A Year in Poems

ROSALIE

FIZZ

BUDDY

BARKLEY

MARILYN SINGER

pictures by
MIKI SAKAMOTO

DIAL BOOKS FOR YOUNG READERS
An imprint of Penguin Group (USA) Inc.

To Oggi, who's always doing something
  —M. Singer

And thanks to Steve Aronson, Stephanie Lurie,
Meredith Mundy, Margaret Woollatt, as well
as the wonderful folks at Dial, especially my
editor, Lucia Monfried

To Jakey, my furry buddy
  —M. Sakamoto

DIAL BOOKS FOR YOUNG READERS
A division of Penguin Young Readers Group

Published by the Penguin Group
Penguin Group (USA) Inc., 375 Hudson Street, New York, New York 10014, U.S.A.
Penguin Group (Canada), 90 Eglinton Avenue East, Suite 700, Toronto, Ontario M4P 2Y3, Canada
    (a division of Pearson Penguin Canada Inc.)
Penguin Books Ltd, 80 Strand, London WC2R 0RL, England
Penguin Ireland, 25 St Stephen's Green, Dublin 2, Ireland (a division of Penguin Books Ltd)
Penguin Group (Australia), 250 Camberwell Road, Camberwell, Victoria 3124, Australia
    (a division of Pearson Australia Group Pty Ltd)
Penguin Books India Pvt Ltd, 11 Community Centre, Panchsheel Park, New Delhi - 110 017, India
Penguin Group (NZ), 67 Apollo Drive, Rosedale, Auckland 0632, New Zealand
    (a division of Pearson New Zealand Ltd)
Penguin Books (South Africa) (Pty) Ltd, 24 Sturdee Avenue, Rosebank, Johannesburg 2196, South Africa
Penguin Books Ltd, Registered Offices: 80 Strand, London WC2R 0RL, England

Published in the United States by Dial Books for Young Readers,
a division of Penguin Young Readers Group
345 Hudson Street, New York, New York 10014
www.penguin.com/youngreaders

Designed by Irene Vandervoort and Sarah Davis
Manufactured in Singapore.

10 9 8 7 6 5 4 3 2 1

    Library of Congress Cataloging-in-Publication Data

Singer, Marilyn.
    Every day's a dog's day : a year in poems / by Marilyn Singer ;
illustrated by Miki Sakamoto. — 1st ed.
        p. cm.
    ISBN 978-0-8037-3715-0 (hardcover)
  1. Dogs—Juvenile poetry. 2. Holidays—Juvenile poetry. 3.
Days—Juvenile poetry. 4. Year—Juvenile poetry. 5. Children's poetry,
American. I. Sakamoto, Miki, ill. II. Title. III. Title: Year in poems.

    PS3569.I546E94 2012
    811'.54—dc22

                          2011021930

Dog Days

Good day, bad day, best day, worst.

   A new ball for fetching, a flea bite—my first.

The park in the spring—look, I found a new path.

   A roll in the mud—oof, I'm getting a bath.

Those long afternoons I sit and I wait.

   Then here comes my girl, and everything's great!

She says, "Fizz! Let's go running! Later we'll rest."

   Good day, bad day, worst day, best.

First Freeze

Hey, Rosalie, come on outside
  so we can play together.
Buddy's here, and Barkley, too.
We really LOVE this weather.
The pavement's cool beneath
  our feet.
This nippy breeze feels nice.
Hey, Rosalie, come on outside—
  just don't slip on that ice!

Snow Day

Better than biscuits,
Better than cake,
Better than burgers
  (no, that's a mistake),
Better than kibble
  or something more sweet
  is licking that white stuff
  right off of the street!

Valentine's Day

Today she calls me "Valentine."
    I know that's not my name.
It doesn't really matter—
    I understand this game.
She hugs me, gives me kisses,
    and something good to gnaw.
She has my heart already,
    so I offer her my paw.

St. Patrick's Day

What does she mean—
   today we wear green?
I don't think that green
   is something I've seen.
She says it's not purple;
   she says it's not blue.
I listen. I sniff.
   I haven't a clue.
But whatever it is,
   in a minute, a few,
I'll bet you a bone
   I'll be wearing it, too.

cead
mile
failte

First Day of Spring

Rosalie, Barkley, Buddy!
Let's roll in something cruddy!
Let's chew up sticks!
Let's pick up ticks!
No dog's a fuddy-duddy!
It's springtime—
      let's get muddy!

Grooming Day

I can tell by her voice
    it's bad news—I've no choice,
    that today is the day
I am doomed.

I can try to refuse,
    hide my leash, chew her shoes.
    It won't work 'cause I'm still
getting groomed.

There's no place I can hide.
    I'll be washed, clipped, and dried.
    And my mistress will say
I look cute.

Then she'll give me a treat,
    and, though that's really sweet,
    can't I smell like a *dog*
and not fruit?

Cat-Chasing Day

It can happen anytime,
  it can happen anyplace.
It's a cause for celebration
  when a feline shows its face.

For a lark you'll charge and bark
  just to get on kitty's case.
With a dissed hiss it'll bristle,
  take a leap, and start to race.

Though you're fast, you'll come in last,
  'cause that cat will set the pace.
Still, you've won because the fun
  is not the finish—

It's the chase!

Birthday Party

Bad party. Barkley
took my ball, and that greedy
pug ate the whole cake.

April Fool's Day

Filling up my favorite bowl
    with fizzy drinks that make me sneeze.
Dangling chewies from a pole,
    hanging biscuits from the trees.

Turning on the TV set
    where noisy beagles jump around.
Laughing when I get upset
    'cause I can't find a single hound.

I still believe you're my best friend.
    I still believe you're pretty cool.
But how I wish this day would end
    so you'll stop saying "April Fool!"

Games Day

TUG-O'-WAR

I've got a stick. You grab an end.
I'm teaching you a game, my friend.
You've got to pull, then pull some more.
That's it—you're playing tug-o'-war!

KEEP AWAY

You see this stick? You want it, don'tcha?
You'll race me fast to get it, won'tcha?
You might just snatch it, if I letcha.
I'll snatch it back and win, I betcha!

Visit to the Vet

Take my leash! Oh, boy! Let's go!
    Someplace new to visit!
A house? A store? A parking lot?
    So tell me, huh, what is it?
Dogs! Dogs! A pack of dogs,
    some quiet and some yappy.
Dogs! Dogs, everywhere–
    I know why they're not happy.
Another room. A table's there.
    It's slippery and high.

Someone's coming through the door.
    Uh-oh, I know this guy.
He checks my belly and my teeth.
    He pokes my front and rear.
I'll never ever like this place.
    Please, let's get out of here!
The sooner we can go back home,
    the sooner I'll forget
this nasty checkup, scary man,
    this visit to the vet!

Graduation Day

Classes end at last today,
    but I flunked "Sit" and I flunked "Stay."
I won't get to celebrate.
    I won't even graduate.
So while my friends are keeping cool,
    tomorrow I start summer school.

First Flea Day

Buddy, Barkley, Rosalie,
  which of you gave me that flea?
I scratch and nibble, roll and gnaw
  to get it off my back, my paw.
Gotcha! Hotcha!
  Wait . . . Oh, brother!
My ear, my rear!
  Here comes ANOTHER!

Pet Parade

Look, I'm wearing a big bow,
   walking slowly in a row.
Where we're going, I don't know.

Listen, drumbeats, banners snapping,
   people cheering, people clapping
(and some pals that can't stop yapping).

Now we cross the railroad track,
  turn around, and walk right back,
still together in a pack.

No one's strayed.

It's a parade!

Fourth of July

Firecrackers popping,
   whistling rockets zooming.
Fireworks exploding,
   cherry bombs ba-booming.

All my people cheer and shout—
   they love that noisy riot.
But if I howl, if I bark,
   they yell, "Hey, you, be quiet!"

First Cookout

Ooh,
   barbecue.

Summer Vacation

Hurry, hurry, throw the ball!
I've been waiting since the fall
    to see it flash, to watch it skim,
    to hear it splash, then plunge
        and swim,
    to grab it, bring it back, and then—
    to make you throw it in again!

Boat Ride

There's nothing for a dog to do
    in this thing called a canoe.

Beach Day

Waves and sand,
   for resting, racing,
    ocean-chasing,
a beach is so grand.

First visit or last,
   for digging, dashing,
    ocean-splashing,
a beach is a blast.

But when you've a thirst
   for tasting, nipping,
    ocean-sipping,
a beach is the worst.

Hole-Digging Day

I must dig a hole
        to look for a mole,
        to bury a bone,
        to lie all alone,
    to—who knows what for?
Then until it's a bore,
        or my paws get too sore,
I must dig ten more.

Last Cookout

Barbecue,
        ooh!

First Day of School

Hot weather,
      always together.
Couldn't last—
      summer's past.
Giggles, grumbles.
      School bus rumbles.

Sit and sigh.
      She's gone—good-bye.
Snooze and wait,
      anticipate.

Distant humming?
      School bus coming!
Once more, carefree—
      she's home with me!

Leaf-Kicking Day

Rosalie, Buddy, Barkley,
let's go! I'm feeling park-ly.
I'll be king of things to fling—
    leaves and twigs, down they'll float,
        settle gently on my coat,
            dangle from my ears and chin.
I'll make everybody grin.
    And, oh yeah, I'll be grinning, too—
it's my favorite thing to do.

Dog Shows

BEST IN SHOW

It's my thing to swing
    around the ring,
to stop, not to budge
    while the judge
checks me out,
to hear the crowd cheer
    when I pose, when I run,
and, especially, when
    I've won.

OBSTACLE COURSE

I can run through any tunnel
    and go over any jump,
fly across a narrow dogwalk
    without falling on my rump,
sail on down a rocky seesaw,
    never frightened by the bump.
I do not care who's watching,
    if I'm worst or if I'm best.
What counts is how I play the game—
    and I play the game with zest.

Halloween

Scary hair
  funny teeth
Rubber face—
  what's underneath?
Shiny wings
  pointy hat
Tail and whiskers—
  that's a cat?
Whoever you're
  supposed to be,
I know your smell—
  you can't fool me!

Thanksgiving

One year I buried the turkey
    and everyone said, "What a shame!"
One year I punctured the football,
    and no one could finish the game.

One year I got in the pantry
    and ate every pie that I found.
So thanks for another Thanksgiving
    and for not sending me to the pound.

Hanukkah

Tasty
potato pan-
cakes under the table.
Then not a latke for
another year.

Christmas

I like the squeaky Santa.
    I like the tennis ball.
I do not mind the sweater
    (though it is a little small).
I do not care about the brush.
    I do not need the brand-new bed.
I do not want those reindeer things
    you stuck upon my head.
I'm happy with a stick to fetch
    and something good to chew.
But most of all I'm glad to get
    one whole long day with you.

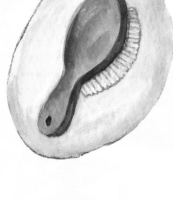

New Year's Day

Good day, bad day, best day, worst.
  She says it's January First!
Brand-new snowflakes, brand-new treat.
  Same good friends I'm glad to meet.
Fresh adventures are in store,
  Plus doing stuff we've done before.
A new year brings—I'll bet you've guessed—
  Each good day, bad day, worst day, best.